PEOPLES OF THE ANCIENT WORLD

Life in

Ancient

Japan

Hazel Richardson

Crabtree Publishing Company
www.crabtreebooks.com

Crabtree Publishing Company

www.crabtreebooks.com

For Edward, Saori, and their wonderful children.

Coordinating editor: Ellen Rodger
Project Editor: Rachel Eagen
Editors: Carrie Gleason, Adrianna Morganelli
Production coordinator: Rosie Gowsell
Production assistance: Samara Parent
Scanning technician: Arlene Arch-Wilson
Photo research: Allison Napier
Art director: Rob MacGregor

Project management:
International Book Productions, Inc.:
Barbara Hopkinson
J. David Ellis
Sheila Hall
Dietmar Kokemohr
Judy Phillips
Janice Zawerbny

Consultant: John S. Brownlee, Ph.D Department of History, University of Toronto

Photographs: Art Archives: p. 14, p. 28 (top); Art Archive/ British Museum: p. 29; Art Archive/ Lucien Biton Collection Paris/ Dagli Orti: p. 30 (bottom); Art Archive/ Musee Cernuschi Paris/ Dagli Orti: p. 16 (top); Art Archive/ Private Collection Paris/ Dagli Orti: p. 10 (bottom), p. 12, p. 22 (bottom); Art Archive/ Victoria and Albert Museum London/ Eileen Tweedy: p. 3, p. 15 (top), p. 18 (bottom); Asian Art and Archaeology, Inc./ Corbis/ Magma: p. 23 (top); Burstein Collection/Corbis/ Magma: p. 25 (top); Comparison of the celebrated beauties and the loyal league/ Fitzwilliam Museum, Univ. of Cambridge, UK/ Bridgeman Art Library: p. 10 (right); Robert Essel NYC/ Corbis/ Magma: p. 9 (top); Mason Florence/ Lonely Planet Images: p. 8 (bottom); Werner Foreman/Corbis/ Magma: p. 24 (bottom); Florence Court, County Femanagh, Northern Ireland/ Bridgeman Art Library: p. 11; Jeremy Hoare/ Almay: p. 20; Hulton- Deutsch Collection/Corbis/ Magma: p. 9 (bottom); Courtesy Japan Studies Institute: p. 25 (bottom); Courtesy JNTO: p. 7 (bottom), p. 19, p. 21 (top), p. 22 (top), p. 24 (top); Kim Kyung-Hoon/Reuters/Corbis: p. 31 (bottom); Chris Lisle/ Corbis/ Magma: p. 18 (top); Craig Lovell/ Corbis/ Magma: pp. 4-5; Kevin R. Morris/ Corbis/ Magma: p. 16 (bottom); Portrait of Izumi Tadahira with a poem, from 'Famous Generals of Japan'/ School of Oriental & African Studies Library, Univ. of London/ Bridgeman Art Library: p. 15 (bottom); Reunion des Musees Nationaux/ Art Resource, NY: p. 21 (bottom); Reuters/ Corbis/ Magma: p. 30 (top); Sakamoto Photo Research Laboratory/ Corbis/ Magma: p. 8 (top), p. 28 (bottom); Shinagawa: departure of Daimyo/ Fitzwilliam Museum, University of Cambridge, UK/ Bridgeman Art Library: p. 17; Liba Taylor/ Corbis: cover; Courtesy Eri U Tokyo: p. 6; Victoria and Albert Museum London/ Eileen Tweedy/ Art Resource, NY: p. 13

Illustrations: William Band: borders, pp.4–5 (timeline), p. 5 (crane), p. 6 (map of Japan), pp. 26–27, p. 30 (shiatsu massage)

Cover: A gilded, or gold-covered, statue of a Japanese *shogun*.

Contents: Woodblock print of a daimyo's attendants watching an archery competition. This print was made by Utagawa Kuniyoshi (1797-1861).

Title page: Samurai trained for many years to become strong warriors.

Crabtree Publishing Company

www.crabtreebooks.com   1-800-387-7650

Cataloging-in-Publication Data
Richardson, Hazel.
   Life in Ancient Japan / written by Hazel Richardson.
      p. cm. -- (Peoples of the ancient world)
   ISBN-13: 978-0-7787-2041-6 (rlb)
   ISBN-10: 0-7787-2041-1 (rlb)
   ISBN-13: 978-0-7787-2071-3 (pbk)
   ISBN-10: 0-7787-2071-3 (pbk)
   1. Japan--Civilization--To 794. 2. Mythology, Japanese. I. Title. II. Series.
DS822.R53 2005
952--dc22

                                        2005001101
                                           LC

Published in the United States
PMB 16A
350 Fifth Ave.
Suite 3308
New York, NY
10118

Published in Canada
616 Welland Ave.
St. Catharines
Ontario, Canada
L2M 5V6

Published in the United Kingdom
73 Lime Walk
Headington
Oxford
OX3 7AD
United Kingdom

Published in Australia
386 Mt. Alexander Rd.
Ascot Vale (Melbourne)
V1C 3032

Contents

Land of Islands

People first settled on the islands that make up Japan 30,000 years ago. It is believed that they may have crossed land bridges that linked the islands to the mainland of Asia. Over time, descendants of these settlers built permanent villages on the coasts. The ancient Japanese called their land Nippon, meaning "land of the rising sun," because they believed the sun rose over their land before any other part of the world.

How Japan Was Created

According to the *Kojiki*, a record of ancient Japanese mythology and history, the Earth was once a shapeless, watery mass. The god Izanagi and the goddess Izanami stirred the waters with a long, jeweled spear. When they pulled the spear out of the water, the water that dripped from the spear thickened and turned into an island. This was the small island of Onokoro. Izanagi and Izanami lived on Onokoro and had many children. The legend states that some of the children turned into the islands of Japan.

▶ *Temples such as the Golden Pavillion in Kyoto, built in 1398, dot the Japanese landscape and are a reminder of Japan's history.*

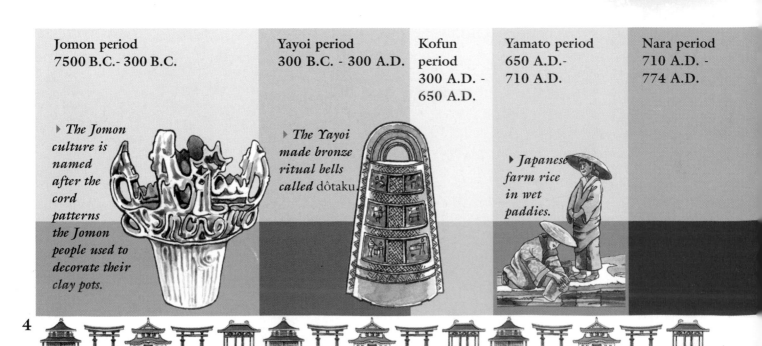

Jomon period 7500 B.C.- 300 B.C.	Yayoi period 300 B.C. - 300 A.D.	Kofun period 300 A.D. - 650 A.D.	Yamato period 650 A.D.- 710 A.D.	Nara period 710 A.D. - 774 A.D.

▶ *The Jomon culture is named after the cord patterns the Jomon people used to decorate their clay pots.*

▶ *The Yayoi made bronze ritual bells called* dôtaku.

▶ *Japanese farm rice in wet paddies.*

The First Peoples

The first peoples of ancient Japan built simple villages. They hunted animals, fished, and gathered wild plants for food. As the population grew, people built larger villages and warehouses to store extra food for trade. They built simple wooden boats and sailed across the East China Sea to trade with the people of ancient Korea and China.

What is a "civilization?"

Most historians agree that a civilization is a group of people that shares common languages, some form of writing, advanced technology and science, and systems of government and religion.

Heian period 794 A.D. - 1192 A.D.	Kamakura period 1192 A.D. - 1333 A.D.	1333 A.D. - 1467 A.D. Muromachi period	Unification period 1568 A.D. - 1602 A.D.	Edo period 1603 A.D. - 1867 A.D.

▼ 1590 A.D. Toyotomi Hideyoshi unites Japan under his rule.

▼ Commodore Perry arrives in Japan in 1853, eventually opening up trade with the West.

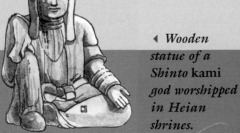

◄ Wooden statue of a Shinto kami god worshipped in Heian shrines.

The Forest Islands

Japan is made up of a chain of volcanic islands in the Pacific Ocean, 120 miles (200 km) from the east coast of China. There are four large islands named Honshu, Shikoku, Kyushu, and Hokkaido, and over 1,000 small ones. The ancient Japanese lived in the mountain valleys and on the coastal plains of the islands.

Earthquakes and Tsunamis

The islands of Japan sit on a **fault line** in the Earth's crust. This has made the land vulnerable to **earthquakes** and volcanic eruptions, which have destroyed villages and left people homeless. Earthquakes also caused tsunamis, or giant waves, that flooded the coasts. Volcanic eruptions left behind lava containing gold, zinc, and copper. The lava enriched the soil and made it fertile for growing food.

▶ *Japan covers 145,840 square miles (377,823 square km). Hokkaido, in the north, lies near the east coast of Russia. Kyushu, in the south, lies southeast of South Korea.*

◀ *According to legend, a giant catfish lived beneath Japan and caused earthquakes by shaking his body. The god Kashima made the land still by trapping the catfish under a rock.*

The Rainy Season

The ancient Japanese planted rice in waterlogged fields between April and May. In early June, a rainy season, called *tsuyu*, began. During *tsuyu*, it rained almost all day, every day, for over a month. *Tsuyu* rains caused landslides and terrible floods in some areas, but also provided the water that food crops, like rice, needed to grow. In the fall, Japan was hit by **typhoons**. These storms damaged crops that had not yet been harvested, and caused more landslides and floods. The northern and western areas of Japan had long, harsh winters with heavy snowfalls. The south and east had milder winters.

Fruits from the Forest, and Sea

The forests of ancient Japan were lush with bamboo, as well as cedar, maple, chestnut, and cherry trees. People used the trees to build houses and temples. They ate budding plants and bamboo **shoots** in the spring, and chestnuts in the fall. Most of their food came from the sea, which was rich with fish like haddock, and other marine life such as shellfish and whales. On the land, people hunted deer, brown bears, foxes, and wild boars for food. They used animal skins to make clothing.

▲ *The Japanese snow monkey slept in trees in winter to stay protected from heavy snowfall.*

▼ *Mount Fuji, at 12,385 feet (3,775 meters), is the tallest mountain in Japan. The ancient Japanese believed it was the dwelling place of Konohana Sakuya Hime, the goddess of flowering trees.*

Workers and Warriors

Most people in ancient Japan lived in small farming communities on land ruled by clans or powerful landowners. Working families shared plots of land and worked together to plant and harvest crops. Many of the ruling families competed for power and had private armies.

The Jomon

About 10,000 years ago, a culture called Jomon developed on the island of Honshu. The culture is named "Jomon," meaning cord pattern, because the people used clay ropes to decorate their pottery. The Jomon peoples learned to craft pots from clay 2,000 years before any other civilization started to make pottery. The Jomon peoples gathered nuts and shoots, hunted deer, and fished for food. By 2500 B.C., the Jomon were farming, using simple stone and wooden tools to work the land. They planted chestnut trees around their villages, and grew millet, a grain they used to make bread.

▲ The Jomon made their pottery by stacking coils of clay, then baking them in a fire until the clay turned hard.

▼ The Jomon built homes by digging pits one foot deep, then surrounding the pits with upright wooden posts. Roofs were made from layers of grass or tree bark. There were up to 700 houses in each Jomon village.

The Yayoi

Archaeologists believe the Yayoi may have come to the island of Kyushu from the Korean peninsula around 300 B.C. The Yayoi brought many new technologies with them. They made pottery on rotating wheels that they turned with their feet. The Yayoi knew how to **forge** bronze and iron into tools and weapons. They also knew how to grow rice in wet fields, or paddies. They carved stepped rice paddies into the sides of steep mountains. These paddies were flooded in the rainy season and drained before harvesting. One acre of rice paddies could feed more people than one acre of any other crop, so rice soon became the major food crop in Japan. Over time, the Yayoi people spread out and settled on the island of Honshu.

▲ *Rice farming became so important in ancient Japan that it changed the way people lived, worked, and were governed.*

The Ainu

The Ainu were among the first peoples to live in Japan. Historians do not know exactly when they arrived in Japan or where they came from. It is believed that they lived on all of the islands but were later driven north by other groups of peoples who settled in Japan. The invaders seized Ainu lands for themselves and treated the Ainu badly because they did not look like most of the people who had settled in Japan. The Ainu lived in small villages and fished, hunted, and farmed wheat, turnip, and millet. They believed in many nature gods, such as the sea god.

▲ *Ainu girls tattooed their lips to protect them from evil spirits. They added on to their tattoos as they grew older.*

Ruling Clans

Rice farming was difficult and required many people to work together in the fields. The land was divided into separate regions, each ruled by a group, or clan, of powerful warriors called an *uji*. By 57 A.D., more than 100 *uji* controlled the land that made up Japan. Most people did not belong to an *uji*. Instead, they belonged to families of workers who lived on the land controlled by an *uji*. The working families were organized by the type of work they did into groups called *be*. The members of a *be* had to work hard to produce goods for their *uji*. This earned them the right to live on the land. Each *uji* had several *be*, including a farming, pottery, weaving, and fishing *be*.

▲ *A family of weavers making cloth.*

▶ *Early Japanese noblewomen wore flowing gowns made of silk. They carried umbrellas to protect their skin from the sun's rays.*

The Yamato

In 250 A.D., a new wave of settlers arrived in Japan, most likely from the Korean peninsula. Among them was a clan called the Yamatai, who were horse-riding warriors with steel swords and iron armor. They introduced the cotton plant to Japan, and brought techniques for spinning and weaving it to make clothing. From 250 A.D. to around 600 A.D., the Yamatai **conquered** many other clans on Honshu and Kyushu. The Yamatai were later called Yamato, and eventually ruled most of Japan. Their **chieftain** declared himself emperor, or supreme leader.

Lords and Nobles

Members of powerful clans served in the emperor's court. The emperor gave them land in return for their loyalty. In 710 A.D., the emperor's court was built at Nara, Japan's first capital city. The emperor divided the land that did not belong to the nobles among the peasants. The emperor and his nobles demanded food and goods from the farmers and **artisans** to support their rich lifestyle. When crops were poor, farmers did not have enough food left over to feed their families, and people starved.

Rise of the Samurai

In 794 A.D., the emperor's court was moved to Heian-kyo, or modern-day Kyoto. The court recruited and trained soldiers for an army commanded by nobles. The army maintained law and order and control over the people. Within 200 years, the army's power weakened. People began to acquire weapons to defend themselves instead of relying on the army. A class of warriors eventually formed, and they called themselves "samurai." The samurai became rich and powerful. They were hired to serve as guards at the emperor's palace, as bodyguards for the nobles or lords, and as police. Samurai practiced fighting skills, including sword fighting, archery, and horseback riding. They believed the greatest act of loyalty to their lord was to die fighting for him. If they lost, were shamed in battle, or if their lord died, samurai killed themselves by slicing their stomachs open. This is called *seppuku*.

Women in Japan

Women enjoyed a high status, or rank, in society during the Yayoi and Yamato periods. They were often rulers of clans or fortune tellers called shamans. Women's status changed when the religion of Buddhism and the teachings of Confucius came to Japan from China around 550 A.D. Both traditions taught that women were less important than men. Women were respected only if they were obedient wives and good mothers. As Buddhism and Confucianism became more important, women lost many of their rights. They could no longer own property or attend school. From 770 A.D. to 1629, there were no women rulers in Japan.

The Warrior's Code

Samurai obeyed a code of conduct called *bushido* that stated that courage and pride were more important than anything else. Even when he was outnumbered and defeat was certain, a warrior was never supposed to turn his back on an enemy or try to escape battle. Samurai wore a piece of colored cloth in battle so their acts of bravery could be reported.

▲ *Samurai wore two swords. The* katana *was a long sword, and the* wakizashi *was short. The word "samurai" means "one who serves."*

The Fearsome Fujiwara

The Fujiwara family, a powerful noble clan, ran Japan's government from 858 A.D. to 1156 A.D. They made their family members **regents**, which were the most powerful government jobs. The Fujiwara used their authority to obtain land and riches and to get rid of their rivals, often by killing them. Women in the Fujiwara clan were often married to the emperor, who could have many wives. The Fujiwara clan held so much power that it was able to retire an emperor whenever it liked.

The Shogun

The Taira were a samurai clan that controlled Japan from 1160 to 1185. They were poor rulers who ignored the needs of the people. Emperors continued to be religious rulers, but they had no real power. The Taira family made all of the emperor's decisions for him.

Around 1180 A.D., a samurai named Minamoto no Yoritomo led a revolt against the Taira clan. This revolt turned into a five-year **civil war** called the Genpei War. Yoritomo won in 1185 and forced the emperor's government to make him its leader. In 1192, he demanded that the emperor give him the title of *shogun*, meaning "barbarian-suppressing general." This title gave Yoritomo the right to act however he needed to keep peace in Japan. As the *shogun*, Yoritomo had more power than the government and emperor, and became the true ruler of Japan. He then set up a type of government called a *bakufu*, or *shogunate*.

The *bakufu* was a military government that controlled the samurai. The emperor and his government of advisors continued to control some of the collection of taxes and the allotment of land to peasants.

▼ *Minamoto no Yoritomo, Japan's first* **shogun,** *fought his first battle at the age of thirteen.*

Powerful Warlords

Yoritomo built a new capital at Kamakura on Honshu once he became *shogun*. This was the start of the Kamakura period. Japan was still divided into territories that were run by landholding families. The heads of these families were warlords who paid samurai to protect their land from enemies. The samurai swore loyalty to their lords. In return, they were given land and government positions.

In 1336, a member of a **rival** clan seized power and became *shogun*. He moved the capital to Kyoto and increased the power of the warlords. The warlords set up armies to keep control over their territories. By 1467 A.D., Japan was divided into dozens of separate territories, with no central control. The War of Onin erupted later that year. It spread through Japan quickly, destroying most of Kyoto. The war ended in 1477, but the warlords, who came to be called *daimyo*, continued to compete with each other to become *shogun*.

▲ *A warlord and his attendants watching an archer at practice.*

Under One Rule at Last

In 1550, a *daimyo* named Oda Nobunaga conquered most of the other *daimyo* and became the *shogun*. He brought almost all of the territories in Japan under his rule before he was killed in 1582. Toyotomi Hideyoshi, the new ruler, completed his work, bringing Japan under one ruler. The emperor continued to perform religious ceremonies at festivals on special occasions, such as rice-planting season.

▶ *By the 1300s, there were 260 powerful warlords in Japan, each ruling his own territory.*

Rice and Trade

Growing rice in wet paddies was so successful that by 100 B.C. there was extra rice for trade with other civilizations. Additional trade goods were made from rice, such as *sake*, or rice wine, and vinegar. Rice became very important to Japan's economy and was used as money for more than 1,000 years.

Valuable Rice

In ancient Japan, a person's wealth was measured in *koku*s. One *koku* was 47 gallons (180 liters) of rice. Peasant taxes were charged in rice, and the government paid its high-ranking workers with it. Rice was eaten with every meal. It was also used to make *sake*, flour, and vinegar. Stalks of rice plants were used to make floor mats, ropes, and sandals.

Trade with China and Korea

A small amount of trade between Japan and China began around 2000 B.C., when Chinese traders sailed across the East China Sea to Japan in wooden canoes. Trade increased greatly after 57 A.D., when Japanese **envoys** were sent to Korea and China. Both the ancient Koreans and the Chinese were interested in Japanese silk, which was used to make beautiful clothing, such as *kimonos*, or robes. Peasants made silk by keeping silk worms under the roofs of their homes. The worms spun silk cocoons that were later harvested and woven into fabric. The ancient Koreans also traded iron and bronze tools in exchange for gold and rice from Japan. The ancient Chinese traded bronze mirrors, bells, swords, and spearheads for gold mined in Japanese mountains, as well as rice.

▲ *The chinese traded goods, such as this bronze mirror, for Japanese gold and other items.*

◀ *Before silk could be spun, the cocoons were soaked in boiling water to loosen the glue that kept the silk threads together.*

Trading Groups

Trade with foreign countries was seen as a way to get wealthy. In 1185, rich artisans established trading groups called *za*s. Each *za* in a lord's territory traded one product, such as *sake*. The *za*s could charge whatever they liked for their products since there was no competition with other traders. The merchants and warlords became very wealthy as trade with other nations continued.

Japanese Coins

The ancient Japanese made purchases using quantities of rice rather than money. The first Japanese coins were made by the Yamato government in 708 A.D. The coins were round and had square holes in the center so they could be threaded onto string like beads. At first, coins were made from copper and silver but were later made from copper only. The coins were not widely used because the government had difficulty getting them to isolated villages. The Japanese people went back to using rice instead of coins to pay for things.

The Kaido Roads

Well-made roads were important to the ancient Japanese because they made it easier for armies and traders to travel across the land. Around 600 A.D., the Japanese started to build a national road network connecting the capital city of Nara, on Honshu, to surrounding towns. The roads, known as *kaidos*, allowed merchants to get to seaports so that they could trade with other merchants from Japan, China, and Korea. The *kaidos* were made of pressed dirt, and many have survived to the present day.

▲ *Ships arrived at the port town Naniwa to unload trade goods onto barges that carried them across the city via canals.*

Religion and Beliefs

The ancient Japanese worshipped gods and goddesses of nature as well as ancestor spirits. Over time, their beliefs evolved into a religion called Shinto. As new peoples settled in Japan, they brought their own faiths and customs and these too spread throughout Japan.

Shinto

Shinto, which means "the way of the gods," was the first religion practiced in Japan. Shinto combined a love of nature with the worship of ancestor spirits, known as *kami*. Shintoists believed that when someone died, his or her spirit lived on as a *kami*. *Kami* were believed to control events, such as the outbreak of disease, when they were angered or ignored. People left gifts of food and drink at small **shrines** in their homes to honor and please the *kami*. Shinto has no official **scriptures** or rules. Followers of Shinto believed that a person's actions were judged as good or bad depending on their intentions.

◀ *Fox* kami *were considered to be messengers of the Shinto god Inari, who protected the rice crop.*

◀ *This painting portrays people worshipping the sun goddess, Amaterasu. The Yamato clan, who believed they were descended from Amaterasu, helped to make the sun goddess the most important* kami *in Japan.*

Buddhism

The religion of Buddhism began in India in 528 B.C. Buddhism is based on the teachings of Siddhartha Gautama, known as the Buddha or "Enlightened One." The Buddha believed that the only way for people to avoid suffering was for them to stop wanting things. The Buddha taught that people could achieve a peaceful state of mind through **meditation**. Buddhism eventually spread through Asia and China and was brought to Japan by a visiting Buddhist **monk** in 552 A.D. Later, rulers sent students, scholars, and monks to China to study Buddhism. Buddhists built temples for worship throughout the countryside. Over time, followers of Shinto adopted some Buddhist beliefs.

Kami Cats

An ancient Japanese myth tells of an emperor traveling in a rainstorm one evening. A cat sitting in a doorway waved to him as he passed. The emperor got off his horse and walked toward the cat. When he reached it, a bolt of lightning struck and killed his horse. The emperor believed the cat was a *kami* and had protected him. To this day, many Japanese believe that cats are helpful *kami*.

Confucianism

Confucius was a Chinese **scholar** who lived from 551 B.C. to 479 B.C. Confucius stated that it was important for people to behave in a dutiful way to their family and society. This meant that a ruler must be kind to his subjects; a father must be kind to his children; a husband must be kind to his wife; an older brother must be kind to his younger brother, and an older friend must be kind to a younger friend. Ancient Japanese adopted Confucianism and modeled their public and family lives on these rules, which were called the Five Right Relationships.

◄ *The Buddha taught that meditation was necessary to develop wisdom. Buddhism was declared Japan's official religion in 594 A.D.*

Shinto Shrines

The ancient Japanese built Shinto shrines, or places of worship, in natural
settings. Shintoists believed that *kami* lived in nature, so the shrines were
built next to waterfalls and rocks and in caves and forest clearings. People
visited the shrines to pray for good luck, to thank the *kami* for their
blessings, and to **reflect**. Most shrines had a garden, a worship hall, and
a *kami* hall for the *kami* to live. A mirror, jade stone, or sword hung
on the wall facing the *kami* hall as a symbol of the *kami*'s presence.
Before entering, visitors washed their hands and mouths in a fountain.
Shintoists believe that cleanliness was necessary for a person to be in a
peaceful state of mind for prayer.

Jomon Pit Burials

The Jomon buried their dead in small pits. The body was laid out with its knees
bent up and a stone was placed against its chest. Clay figures of women, which
are believed to be **fertility** goddesses, were sometimes laid around the body.

Yayoi Group Graves

The Yayoi people buried their dead in large clay urns or heavy stone coffins.
Graves were grouped together and marked with a heap of earth or a circle of
stones. Rulers' graves were surrounded by a ditch to separate them from the
commoners' graves. Possessions such as swords, beads, and mirrors were
placed inside the ruler's coffin, so they could be used in the **afterlife**.

▲ *A male Shinto* kami *carved from wood.* Kami *statues were kept in Shinto shrines.*

▼ *All Shinto shrines have a* torii *gate, sometimes painted orange, at the entrance to the complex. Two stone lions or dogs stand guard on either side of the entrance.*

Yamato Mound Burials

Members of ruling families of the Yamato clan were buried in huge mounds of earth, called *kofun*. Later, *kofun* were keyhole-shaped. The dead person was placed in a small room in the mound, along with iron swords, arrowheads, tools, armor, and bracelets that the dead would need in the afterlife. Thousands of clay statues of humans, animals, and buildings were placed on top of the *kofun*. These statues are called *haniwa*. Historians do not know why they were put on graves.

Burning the Dead

Buddhists believed that death was unclean, so they cremated, or burned, their dead. When Buddhism arrived in Japan, people began to practice cremation. After a body was cremated, relatives of the dead lifted a piece of bone from the ashes and placed it in a white pottery jar as a symbol that they had not abandoned the body. A funeral ceremony was held over the next 49 days, after which the bone was buried in a cemetery.

Ancient Fortune-telling

The *Kojiki*, the first Japanese book of myths and history, describes many ways of divination, or telling the future. Fortune-telling was important to the ancient Japanese, who believed that there were good and bad times for certain actions, such as going to war. Divination was used to find out when the best time to act was. The most common method of divination was to write a question, such as what the next season's weather or outcome of crops would be like, on a turtle shell or a cow's shoulder blade bone. Then the bone was heated until it cracked. A diviner studied the shape of the crack, then interpreted it as either a positive or negative answer to the question.

▼ **Haniwa** *have been found all over Japan.* **Haniwa** *may be in the shape of humans and animals, or articles such as fans and weapons.*

Language and Learning

The ancient Japanese borrowed a system of writing from China, their neighbor to the west, and altered it to suit their own language. Over time, three different styles of writing developed in Japan.

Writing

Chinese writing was introduced to Japan around 500 A.D. At first, the Japanese language was written using Chinese **characters**, but the **script** slowly changed to reflect the Japanese language. Japanese words are written according to sounds rather than letters. For example, two or three English letters might be combined to create one Japanese sound. This sound is expressed as one symbol, or character. Three types of writing systems were used in ancient Japan. The first was called *kanji*. In *kanji*, Japanese words were written using Chinese characters. Around 800 A.D., a script based on the way Japanese syllables sounded, called *hiragana*, developed. *Hiragana* was a simplified version of *kanji*. The Japanese called it "women's hand" since mostly women used it at first. *Katakana* was a script first used by Buddhist monks, students, and men. It was based on Japanese syllables, so the writer did not need to know Chinese to use the script.

▲ *"Hospitality" written in* hiragana.

▶ *Murasaki Shikibu, author of one of Japan's most famous books, the* Genji Monogatari.

Poetry

Traditional Japanese poetry is based on patterns of syllables. It does not have to rhyme. Early Japanese poems, called *tanka*, always had 31 syllables and were meant to make the reader feel one emotion. Today, the most famous style of Japanese poetry is *haiku*, which is a three-line poem with 17 syllables. The first collection of Japanese poetry was the *Manyoshu*, or *Collection of Myriad Leaves*. Some of these poems express the Japanese love for nature, and sadness for all beautiful things, because they must die eventually.

Going to School

Only the **privileged** went to school in ancient Japan. Children from noble families were taught to read and write. They also studied math, history, poetry, and government. Children were taught by Confucian scholars and by Buddhist priests. Peasant children did not go to school, but they learned their parents' work by helping them. They learned trades such as making paper, pottery, and silk, and learned to plant and harvest rice.

Literature

The *Kojiki*, or the *Record of Ancient Matters*, was the first Japanese book written in 712 A.D. Between 794 and 1195, most of Japan's great writers were women. One of Japan's most famous books is the *Genji Monogatari*, meaning *Tale of Genji*, written around 1120 A.D. by Murasaki Shikibu. She lived in the emperor's court and wrote stories about the power struggles between the noble ladies who lived there. Genji, the hero of the story, is the emperor's son and goes through many struggles to find love.

▲ *This woman is the subject of a* **tanka** *poem, which is written at the top right of the picture.*

▸ *The abacus was a counting instrument that school children used for solving math problems.*

Arts and Culture

Many Japanese art forms came from China between 650 A.D. and 1000 A.D. The Japanese adapted these forms over hundreds of years into styles that reflect the Japanese interest in nature and drama.

The Tea Ceremony

Chanoyu, the tea ceremony, was brought to Japan by Buddhist monks from China around 800 A.D. *Chanoyu* was seen as a way to make daily life more beautiful, and eventually became a major part of Japanese culture. The tea ceremony was often included in religious ceremonies. Tea houses were built on stilts and surrounded by beautiful gardens.

Origami

Origami is the art of folding paper. It has been practiced in Japan since 500 A.D. Paper was folded into shapes that had symbolic meaning and were used in Shinto ceremonies. The paper was imported from China and was expensive, so only the wealthy did *origami* at first. Once the Japanese learned to make paper, it was used to sculpt useful objects, such as boxes and wallets.

Noh Theater

Noh theater developed in Japan around 1350. The plays told stories about *kami*, love, and battles between heroes and evil spirits. The actors wore painted wooden masks instead of makeup. Only men were allowed to perform in noh plays. The actors recited poetry accompanied by music made with drums and flutes.

▲ The tea master adds boiling water to powdered green tea, called matcha, *then whisks the mixture until it is frothy.*

▼ Noh actors wore different masks to show the changing emotions of their characters.

Making Washi

Buddhist monks brought papermaking technology to Japan from China around 610 A.D. The Japanese adapted the technique to make their own type of paper, called *washi*. First, stalks of the gampi shrub were boiled in water. Once they had softened, the bark was removed and the outer bark was discarded. The inner bark was beaten into a pulp with wooden paddles, then poured into tubs full of water and vegetable gum, a thick liquid that made the pulp stick together. After several days, the pulp was spread onto screens and dried in the sun to make sheets of paper.

Flower Arranging

Ikebana means the "way of the flower." Buddhist monks in China studied ways of arranging flowers, leaves, and branches to make beautiful arrangements that helped them meditate. When the monks came to Japan, they brought their flower arranging methods with them. *Ikebana* was usually practiced as a pleasant way of passing the time by the upper classes of ancient Japan.

Yamato-e Painting

Around 800 A.D., the Japanese developed a style of painting known as *yamato-e*. These were detailed landscapes showing beautiful areas of Japan. *Yamato-e* painting was used to decorate sliding screens that separated rooms in the homes of nobles. They also illustrated stories in books.

▲ *A yamato-e painting shows a ruler sitting in a beautiful landscape.*

▼ *Ikebana is meant to show the relationship between the sky, Earth, and people.*

Life of a Warrior

Some of the greatest achievements in weaponry were developed from the need for people to defend themselves in ancient Japan. Samurai learned to become strong warriors by training many long and difficult hours. Samurai served under powerful warlords and lived with their families in fortress-like compounds.

1. Samurai began training at the age of five or six. They practiced with wooden swords before they were given a steel sword. Samurai trained for hours, often in physical pain, to develop the strong mind of a warrior. They meditated and fasted, or went for long periods without eating food.

2. Samurai had to be very skilled to shoot bows and arrows, so they practiced all the time. They were famous for being able to shoot a bow and arrow while riding a horse.

3. Bows, first used around 250 A.D., were made of bamboo and were about six feet (two meters) long. Eagle, hawk, or crane feathers were glued to an arrow to make it fly in a straight line. The ancient Japanese invented two types of arrowheads: a four-sided arrowhead that could pierce armor, and a three-pronged arrowhead that could cut rope. A whistle was sometimes attached to the arrow's shaft to signal the attack as it sailed through the air.

4. Swords were more than weapons to the ancient Japanese. They were thought to have powers and lives of their own, their strength and magic affected by the thoughts and actions of the swordsmith. A swordsmith fasted while he worked so he would be pure and the sword he made would be more powerful.

5. Samurai wives had to know how to defend their homes in wartime. They carried a dagger and knew how to fight with a curved sword on a long pole, called a *naginata*.

Friend or Foe?

Japan's location in the Pacific Ocean helped to protect it against enemies because it was surrounded by water and could only be reached by ship. Japan faced only two foreign invasions and both were unsuccessful.

The Mongol Hordes

A group of **nomadic** warriors called the Mongols spread across Asia around 1200. Under their ruler, Genghis Khan, the Mongols conquered northern China, Russia, central Asia, and Persia. In 1260, Genghis Khan's grandson, Kublai Khan, became the leader of the Mongols.

Mongol Invasion

When Kublai Khan demanded that Japan pay a tax to China in 1268, Japan refused. Kublai Khan prepared to invade. Six years later, 900 warships armed with **catapults** and gunpowder bombs sailed for Japan, with 40,000 Mongol, Chinese, and Korean soldiers onboard. They landed on Kyushu, where Japanese samurai fought to defend their island. Salvation came when a typhoon struck, killing thousands of the invaders, and destroying 200 ships docked on shore. The Mongols retreated. The next year, Kublai Khan sent a messenger to Japan, once again demanding that they pay a tax to China. The Japanese sent back the messenger's head. The Mongols invaded Japan again in 1281 and killed thousands of people. When another typhoon struck, it destroyed hundreds of Mongol ships, and forced them back to China.

▲ *Kublai Khan set up court in Beijing, China after coming to power. He conquered Korea before setting his sights on Japan.*

◄ *The Japanese believed that the typhoon storms that stopped two Mongol invasions were sent by a storm god to protect them. They called the typhoons* kamikaze, *which means "divine wind."*

28

European Contact

Europeans first landed in Japan in 1543, when shipwrecked Portuguese soldiers washed up on Japan's shores. Japanese merchants eagerly began trading with the Portuguese for their guns. In 1600, Dutch ships arrived at Kyushu and started to trade with the Japanese. Holland and Japan continued to trade for 250 years.

Retreat into Isolation

As trade between Japan and Europe opened up, Japan began to change. European traders brought their own customs, threatening Japanese traditions and beliefs. In the 1630s, the Japanese government banned most foreign trade. European ships were no longer allowed to dock at Japanese ports, except for a few Dutch ships. Japan's isolation from western countries lasted 251 years.

End of Isolation

In 1853, four U.S. warships commanded by Commodore Perry anchored off Edo Bay, on the east coast of Japan. The commodore brought with him a letter from the U.S. president requesting that Japan sign a **treaty** to open its ports to trade with the United States. Perry promised to return the next spring for an answer. The Japanese agreed to the treaty and two ports were opened to the Americans. Small amounts of trade continued into the following year. In 1858, Russia, Britain, the Netherlands, and France made similar trade treaties with Japan, and four more ports were opened for foreign trade. Japan's isolation had finally ended.

▼ *When Commodore Perry first arrived in Japan, the Japanese thought the United States was invading their country.*

Ancient Traditions

Many of the cultural traditions of ancient Japan continue to be practiced today. Traditional Japanese entertainment, sports, and martial arts remain important in modern-day Japan. Other aspects of Japanese culture have become popular in many parts of the world.

Geisha

In ancient Japan, geisha were women who performed music and dance in tea houses and inns. They first appeared during the Heian period, and were most popular from the 1600s to the 1800s. It took many years to become a geisha. Girls often began training when they were seven years old. They were educated in Japanese arts such as dancing, music, the tea ceremony, *ikebana*, poetry, and conversation. Since married women were expected to remain in the home, a geisha had to give up her career if she wanted to marry.

▶ *Geisha continue to wear beautiful silk kimonos and decorative hairstyles.*

▼ *Shiatsu massage was brought to North America, where it remains a popular therapy.*

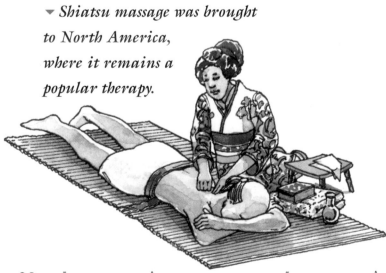

Herbal Medicine and Massage

The ancient Japanese made **poultices**, **ointments**, and teas from plants and herbs known for their healing properties. Rhubarb was used to treat burns, while ginger was used for nausea. Headaches and back pain were treated with a special massage technique called shiatsu. Shiatsu was developed from the belief that invisible streams of energy move through the body. Some Japanese believed that illnesses were caused when the flow of energy was blocked. During a shiatsu massage, an expert pressed on different parts of the body to help the energy flow more easily.

Ancient Fighting Techniques

Jujitsu is a style of fighting that developed in Japan over a 2,500-year period. By the 1600s A.D. it was a key part of samurai training. Using knowledge of the body's weak spots, a samurai used throws and kicks to take down his opponent. *Jujitsu* developed into *judo* in the 1800s, and is practiced all over the world today. *Kendo* was inspired by samurai sword fighting, but a bamboo stick is used to defend an attack rather than a samurai sword. *Karate* is the Japanese art of self-defense, and has become very popular in North America.

Sumo Wrestling

The first history of Japan, the *Kojiki*, tells of how two men battled with each other for the ownership of Japan over 2,500 years ago. They fought each other using a style of fighting called sumo wrestling. In sumo matches, opponents grapple with each other in a ring. The first wrestler who is pushed out of the ring loses. Sumo wrestlers weighed up to 400 pounds (180 kg) and were extremely strong. Today, sumo wrestling is Japan's national sport and the best wrestlers are rich and famous. They are treated as heroes.

▲ *A young Japanese samurai carried a stick, bow, arrows, and two swords. He was trained in several fighting styles to be a fearsome opponent, even without weapons.*

◄ *Modern sumo wrestlers enter the ring wearing decorated aprons.*

Glossary

afterlife A life believed in many religions to continue after death

archaeologist A scientist who studies human history by examining fossils and old buildings

artisan A person skilled in making products, such as pottery or jewelry

catapult A machine that throws large objects, such as stones

character A letter of the alphabet

chieftain The leader of a clan

civil war A war between two groups of people from the same nation

clan A group of people who belong to the same family

compound A house or group of houses surrounded by a barrier

conquer To take over by force

descendants People who share a family history

earthquake When the Earth shakes as the edges of two rocky plates that make up the Earth's crust move against each other along the fault line

envoy A person who is sent by one government or ruler to meet with another government or ruler

fault line A line of weakness in the Earth's crust

fertile Able to produce life

forge The art of shaping metal into objects

meditate The act of thinking quietly

monk A person who devotes his or her life to a religion and lives in a monastery

nomadic Moving from place to place

ointment A healing substance applied to the skin

poultice A thick, healing paste that is placed on a cut or swollen part of the body

privileged Someone who has a special advantage

reflect To think about one's life or experiences

regent Someone who acts in the place of a ruler

rival An enemy

scholar An expert on one or many topics

script Writing

scriptures Sacred or holy writings or books

shoot New growth on a plant

shrine A place that is devoted to a god or gods to honor them

slave A person who is owned by another person

tax Money demanded by a government from its people

treaty An agreement made between one or more nations or rulers

typhoon A heavy rainstorm with strong winds

Index